0863815

Gallery Books
Editor Peter Fallon

LAMENT FOR ART O'LEARY

Vona Groarke

LAMENT FOR ART O'LEARY

from the Irish of
Eibhlín Dubh Ní Chonaill

Gallery Books

Lament for Art O'Leary
is first published
simultaneously in paperback
and in a clothbound edition
on 26 April 2008.

The Gallery Press
Loughcrew
Oldcastle
County Meath
Ireland

www.gallerypress.com

*All rights reserved. For permission
to reprint or broadcast this work,
write to The Gallery Press.*

© Vona Groarke 2008

ISBN 978 1 85235 444 2 *paperback*
     978 1 85235 445 9 *clothbound*

A CIP catalogue record for this book
is available from the British Library.

the arts council
chomhairle
ealaíon

LAMENT FOR ART O'LEARY

Introduction

1773. In America things are coming to a head between the Colonists and the British Government: the Boston Tea Party will take place in December. The first book published by an African-American is Phillis Wheatley's *Poems on Various Subjects, Religious and Moral.* In Dublin Lord Edward Fitzgerald is being raised on Rousseau's principles in Frascati House. The Casino at Marino and the Grand Canal are under construction. Edward Bunting, who will transcribe at the Belfast Harp Festival in 1792 most of what we now know as traditional Irish harp music, is born. Eoghan Rua Ó Súilleabháin, the last great Irish poet of the eighteenth century, is tutoring the children of the Nagle family and eyeing up their mother. The new Lord Lieutenant of Ireland, Lord Harcourt, proposes a tax on absentee landlords. Charles Vallancey publishes his *Grammar of the Iberno-Celtic, or Irish Language* in which he characterizes Irish as 'masculine' and 'nervous', akin to Persian and Chinese. James Cooper Walker is gathering material for his *Historical Memoirs of the Irish Bards* and Charlotte Brooke, who in 1789 will publish her *Reliques of Irish Poetry* (the first anthology to publish original Irish poems alongside their English translations), is learning Irish after hearing one of her father's farm labourers read from a manuscript. Elizabeth Ryves, 'descended from a family of distinction in Ireland' (according to an obituary in 1797), is working on a ballad that will be published in her *Poems on Several Occasions* (1777), whose first two lines read: 'Ye subjects of Britain, attend to my song / For, to you both, the Muse and her numbers belong.' On May 5th, King George III and Queen Charlotte attend a Royal

Command performance of Oliver Goldsmith's *She Stoops To Conquer* in London's Covent Garden Theatre. On that same night, in Rathleigh House near Macroom in County Cork, the body of Art O'Leary, shot down in a field the day before, is being waked by his widow and sister. The keen, or funeral lament, that they extol over him will, two centuries later, in 1984, be described by Peter Levi in his inaugural lecture as Professor of Poetry at Oxford as 'the greatest poem written in these islands in the whole eighteenth century'.

From the day in November 2006, on a train from Aldeburgh to London, that Peter Fallon suggested I have a go at translating Eibhlín Dubh Ní Chonaill's *Chaoineadh Airt Uí Laoghaire* (Eileen O'Connell's *Lament for Art O'Leary*), I've been wondering what I have to bring to this astonishing poem. My first reaction was that my Irish isn't good enough to dare a new translation. But then (because I badly wanted to do it and didn't mind coming up with all kinds of reasons why I should!) I thought that maybe I could do a version that admits it considers English translations as much as it concentrates on the original.

Eileen's lament is a wellspring for Irish poetry in the English language: writers as diverse as Eleanor Hull, Frank O'Connor, John Montague, Thomas Kinsella, Eilís Dillon, Brendan Kennelly, Sean Ó Tuama, Patrick Galvin, James Simmons, Michael Smith and Paul Muldoon have all written versions of all or part of it. Scholars too have taken it on, with translations by P L Henry and, most recently, Angela Bourke who made a fine translation in Volume IV of the *Field Day Anthology of Irish Literature* (Cork University Press, 2002) alongside a valuable introductory essay. Declan Kiberd devotes a chapter to the Lament in his *Irish*

Classics (Granta Books, 2000) and Sean Ó Tuama has also written wonderfully about it in his 1995 collection of essays, *Repossessions* (Cork University Press, 1995).

The Lament has made its presence felt in Irish culture in other ways also. Dermot Bolger's play, *The Lament for Arthur Cleary*, reimagines the original and transplants it to contemporary Dublin. Tom Mac Intyre too has used it as the basis for his play, *Caoineadh Airt Uí Laoghaire*. It has even made its way onto the silver screen, in Bob Quinn's 1975 film (also named *Caoineadh Airt Uí Laoghaire*, starring a fresh-faced Seán Bán Breathnach), and into music in 2002 with a setting by Peadar Ó Riada and the Cór Ban Chúil Aodha. Seamus Heaney paid tribute to it in an essay he wrote for the *Guardian* (November 2005) about his writing of *The Burial at Thebes* (2004) in which he noted, 'A tuning fork sounded when I remembered the opening lines . . . This stricken, urgent keen for a murdered husband, beaten out in line after three-stressed line, gave me the note I needed for the anxious, cornered Antigone at the start of the play.'

I have read and studied all the versions I could find. While working on the translation I kept the Irish version of Eileen's lament, quoted by Angela Bourke, beside me, along with translations by O'Connor, Ó Tuama and Kinsella. My own version of the poem is based on no single English-language source but, rather, on as many as I could locate. If I had found in any one of them absolutely everything I wanted in a translation I wouldn't have persisted with my own. O'Connor's (which I love for its grace of feeling and elegance of expression) jigs around uncertainly and loses ground in the final movements. Bourke's more matter-of-fact scholarly translation (quite rightly) values faithfulness to the original Irish above all. Dillon's, Kinsella's and Montague's are shortened versions that dispense with the complicated issues around additions and asides to the main text. Some translators go for a resoundingly contemporary vocabulary, others allow for a tone which honours its historical provenance.

In her Introduction to the section 'Lamenting the Dead' in the *Field Day Anthology* Angela Bourke suggests that, 'To the extent that it offers women a licence to speak loudly and without inhibition, and frequently to defend their own interests against those of men, *caoineadh* may be read as feminist utterance.' Perhaps English, with its feminine decorums, has been more inclined to quieten down Eileen's immoderate passions. Or perhaps Irish is a better language for giving vent to grief.

Or it may be that translating a poem that is partly prescribed by a tradition that has no real equivalent in English raises difficulties of tone and register. But most versions, I think, fail to capture completely the extremes of Eileen's rage and desire. What is missing, perhaps, has been a version in English that tried to nail how much Eileen really *fancied* her husband. If I have sacrificed accuracy for passion, the defence I offer rests in my understanding of my version as an attempt to capture the *tone*, as opposed to the exact *content*, of the original Irish.

Eileen's is an unusual lament: it has a curious, hybrid provenance. Traditionally, the lament was intoned by several, professional keening women over the body of the deceased. On their account of a visit to Ireland, published as *Ireland: Its Scenery and Character* (How and Parsons, 1841), Mr and Mrs Samuel Hall observed a wake:

The women of the household range themselves at either side, and the keen at once commences. They rise with one accord, and, moving their bodies with a slow motion to and fro, their arms apart, they continue to keep up a heart-rending cry. This cry is interrupted for a while to give the ban caointhe (the leading keener), an opportunity of commencing. At the close of every stanza, the cry is repeated . . . and then dropped; the woman then again proceeds with the dirge, and so on to the close.

Eileen's is not a typical keen in that it has an identified author rather than an anonymous or even a collective source. It also has a very definite sense of taking the tradition of the keen onto a whole new level of personal articulation, moving it much closer to our idea of a one-off, authored poem. And it is an unusual poem in that it wasn't made as most poems are, with a degree of forethought: rather, it was extemporized for performance, in the tradition of the public lament. And it wasn't written down until thirty years after it was composed, and then not by Dark Eileen herself.

Yet Eileen's lament strikes me as deliberate and artful: although extemporized it exists at the meeting point of a cultured imagination and a cultural inheritance. It is not a folk poem in the way that 'The Sean Van Vocht' or 'The Croppy Boy' are orally transmitted folk poems with close links to music and politics. Certainly it is highly stylized, formal and aware of its heritage. (Angela Bourke notes the parallels and crossovers with other keens of the period.) But what makes the poem remarkable is the singularity of Eileen's voice, the moments when a flicker of vivid expression remind us that this is the achievement of a distraught, educated, complicated and haughty woman. Eileen is more than the product of her historical and cultural moment: however much we ask her to she cannot be pressed to speak only of her class and Gaelic tradition. Instead, she does what all poets do: with a glance backwards and a hard look inwards she makes of immediacy and impulse a form of words that speaks across context and tradition to attest to the intensity of its living moment.

Taking on a project like this raises inevitable difficulties. How do you take something from one tradition and apply it to, or find a place for it in, another? The keen doesn't bend easily to the decorums of English. Sometimes I found that my 'translation' of lines had squeezed the life out of them. At other times I had to add an image or a metaphor to try to give a passage an inkling of the elegance or music that I recognized in the Irish.

And how do you 'make it new'? Sometimes I had to be drastic. The opening line of Eileen's lament in the Irish version, 'Mo ghrá go daingean tú!' (one of the most familiar lines of poetry in Irish), has been translated variously as 'My love and my delight' (O'Connor), 'My love forever!' (Ó Tuama, Dillon, Montague), 'Beloved' (Galvin), 'Dear firm friend' (Bourke), 'My closest and dearest' (Hull) and 'My steadfast love' (Kinsella). In truth, these endearments were what I found hardest to translate. They sound different in English, a little phony to my ear, and also, despite their intention, off-puttingly formal. Instead I have used the simple (and lovely) word 'Husband' which seemed to me more intimate than the more lavish alternatives.

I had to dispense with the three-beat line that suited Seamus Heaney's purpose. Over prolonged stanzas, in English, it became monotonous and stale. I was sorry to lose it, but maintaining it demanded a sacrifice of drama and sincerity that I felt, in the end, was too high a price to pay. I suppose the treads and risers of poetry are different language by language: I think the power of Eileen's proclamation lies in the high-wire tension between the music of its art, the unrelenting steady nerve of it, and the extremes of passion contained therein.

I've taken the licence of reattributing to Eileen two sections given by Ó Tuama to Art's father. It was the only time this man spoke, and what he said was very close in spirit and tone to Eileen's sections that preceded and followed. Acknowledging this third (vague and momentary) presence seemed to me an unnecessary distraction from the drama and tension of the women's verbal contests.

So, who were the people at the centre of the poem and from where does the drama derive? Eileen's was an important Irish family — she was an aunt of Daniel O'Connell. Her mother kept up one of the few big Gaelic houses to survive under English rule and, although the family's first language was Irish (Eileen's mother was herself a noted poet), the children were tutored in Latin, French and English. In *Repossessions* Ó Tuama claims that the O'Connells were in fact 'living or endeavouring to live as if the old Irish aristocratic order had not collapsed nearly two centuries previously'. It seems likely that a large-scale smuggling operation between south Kerry and the European mainland allowed them to maintain considerable wealth.

Eileen's first marriage to O'Connor of Iveragh left her a widow at the age of fifteen. (It is said that Eileen sat cracking nuts during this gentleman's wake!) When she first laid eyes on Art O'Leary at the market in Macroom some seven years later she set her cap at him.

He was a young captain home on leave from the Hungarian Hussars, mounted on a splendid mare and bearing a sword in public, an act expressly forbidden to Catholics under the Penal Laws.

He was also probably one of the last men a family who had good reason to conduct its affairs with discretion and a degree of anonymity would have chosen for Eileen. When she eloped with Art in 1767 the O'Connells broke off all contact with her. Eileen's brother, Daniel, referred in a letter to Art's 'ungovernable temper'. Six years later, not one of her family would attend Art's funeral. The couple lived together in the O'Leary family home, Rathleigh House near Macroom. That house, still occupied, has a large stable yard under which Art's brown mare is said to be buried, having been shot by Eileen in a fit of rage after Art's death.

Art was flamboyant and headstrong, a right young buck. He must have been good-looking: from Eileen's descriptions we know he dressed well and carried himself with assurance and perhaps a little too much pride. Certainly he wasn't shy about baiting the English authorities. The recorded facts suggest the following sequence of events:

Not long after Art's marriage the High Sheriff of Macroom, Abraham Morris, has a falling-out with him. To put Art in his place Morris invokes the Penal Law against a Catholic owning a horse worth more than five pounds and demands that Art sell him the valuable mare for this amount. Art duly refuses and one of Morris's servants fires at him. In anger O'Leary seizes Morris's gun, an act which puts him firmly on the wrong side of the law. He is declared 'notoriously infamous' by Morris who, in 1771, offers a reward for his arrest.

Their ongoing feud comes to a head on May 4, 1773. Art, tired of the fugitive life, determines to kill Morris. A local farmer called Cooney relays his intention to Morris who instead gathers a company of soldiers to run him down. Art escapes them and is resting in a field at Carriginima when he is shot dead. His beloved mare gallops the seven miles home to Eileen. Eileen mounts the horse which takes her to where her husband's body lies bleeding by the side of the road. She cups her hand in his blood and drinks from it, and begins to intone the first part of her keen.

Art O'Leary's body was buried first in a common field (Morris having invoked another Penal Law which forbade him burial in the O'Leary family plot) and then six months later was transferred to Kilcrea church-yard where the inscription on his headstone still reads 'generous, handsome and brave'. It is believed that the poem accumulated when Eileen and Art's sister waked his body and was subsequently added to when Art was re-interred. This could certainly account for differences of tone throughout the poem where the latter sections seem to have a resignation and a more extensive sense of ongoing grief than is compatible with the extremes of emotion expressed in the first two-thirds.

The keen was a public act. One, or several, of the group of mourners (keeners) memorized Eileen's lament and thus preserved it in oral form. Twice it was written down from recitations by a professional keening woman, Norrie Singleton; once around 1800 and again, shortly before her death at a great age, around 1870. The similarities between Singleton's versions suggest that she hadn't been adding sundry personal touches to the version she gave thirty years after Art's death and that, as Ó Tuama writes, her versions, particularly the first, are 'a close approximation to Eileen Dubh's original lament'. Other recollected additions to and versions of Eileen's lament were collected around Cork and Kerry in the nineteenth century and are housed in the Folklore Collection at University College, Dublin. Untangling what was actually incanted over Art's body from what might have been is an impossible task. Ó Tuama based his translation on the first of Singleton's versions, Bourke on the second, with lines added by Patrick Ferriter from a version he heard from a relative, Margaret Finnegan, in Tralee in 1893.

As the old joke has it, the keen is a dying art. In that it is no longer practised as a funeral rite, it is a dead art, but Eileen O'Connell's lament remains a living thing. It has survived and, as we read it, we become a part of that survival. Picking any line and saying it aloud means we give breath to words that first passed over the lips of Dark Eileen O'Connell as she bent over her husband's stretched body in May of 1773. That those words were in Irish and that they are not these same words we have to bear in mind. But insofar as we can ever enter a moment in lives that are not our own, or a language that many of us no longer practise; insofar as we can inhabit any other person's grief or grievance; insofar as poetry can ever speak to us across the ditches of centuries, Eileen's lament allows us. It turns the here and now around to face another time and place, so that we almost stand beside her and feel the heat of her outrage on our own cheeks.

The urgency, passion and elegance of Eileen's utterance throw themselves against a darkness we can't fail to recognize. We are moved, yes, not only by the sheer force of a tradition that knew how to launch itself into that desolation, but also by the single voice of a pregnant widow that calls up her husband in his hand-stitched shoes to stand again before her. Who among us, having encountered Eileen's vision of Art on his horse and having realized the power of both her desire and her art, is likely to forget it?

Vona Groarke

Lament for Art O'Leary

EILEEN

Husband,
when you stood out that market day
my eyes settled on you.
I knew I would have you
if it meant
stepping out of my whole life,
carrying nothing with me.

Not that that mattered anyway.
You led me through rooms
that whitened as we walked,
had a blaze of comforts stoked for me
whenever I desired.
You shook out your house for me,
had bedrooms chastened
and kitchens stacked.
You had mackerel hooked for me,
lambs fattened on silky grass for me,
loaves shaped like the sun and moon for me
and women on hand to see to it all,
to pour and knead and clean.
All I had to do was turn over
in my hand-spun nets of sleep.

My dear,
I picture you with sunlight
tied around your head
like a band of gold,
every crease and angle of you —
from your silver-hilted sword
to your fine-trimmed mount —

a compliment to that spring day
and what it had to offer you.
Even the English lowered their eyes
from the vision of you
on your foreign horse.
Not that that mattered in the end:
it wasn't their eyes that undid you.

You were every inch the heir
of the Earls of Antrim
and the upright Barrys of Imokilly,
but you were still
the footloose suckling calf
that had warmed
my breasts that morning.

My white-gloved horseman,
I'd have watched you forever
in your cambric and laces,
your worsted and leather,
your hand-stitched shoes
and your Austrian breeches
that showed off your
sleek, powerful thighs
astride the brown mare
that was a match for you
in vigour and elegance.

My soft-fingered Art,
the light glinting off
your golden brooch
reached me all the way

over the sea.
And when you followed
in your finery
I thought that selfsame
blaze of yours
would blind
even the English
in our streets.
Not that it mattered in the end:
it wasn't their eyes that undid you.

My love,
when I go back home to them
little Conor and the stripling, Fiach,
will ask what I have done with you,
where I have hidden their father.
I will have to find words to say to them
that you are not hidden and you are not hiding
unless it is in Kilnamartyr,
from where no father comes home.

My Art,
I wouldn't give the time of day
to rumour of your death
until that selfsame mare of yours
came to me with her bridle awry,
her withers smattered
with your heart's damson,
and the polished saddle,
where I last saw you bolt upright,
lopsided and bereft.

My first spurt
took me clean over
your side of the bed.
The second got me to the gate,
the third up on her back.
I slapped my hands
to set her going
and she took off
at a heedless pace
that didn't spill one second
until she carried me
to the single furze
where your dear body
slumped.

No priest was on hand
to whisper prayers,
no monk to sing your praises,
only a dry-eyed, sorry, old woman
to throw a bare coat over you.
Art O'Leary,
I knelt down beside you.
I plunged my two fists
in your spilled blood
and sucked from my useless fingers.

Husband,
get up and follow me home.
I'll have dinner made for you
of venison and claret.
I'll fill the house
with your admirers.

I'll have music played for you.
When you've had your fill of that
I will turn down a bed for you
of cashmere blankets and speckled quilts
to draw the cold out of your bones
that this north wind has frozen.

ART'S SISTER
My treasure,
not a single woman
from Cork to Toames
with her money to hand
and a purse to offer
would have chosen to refuse you.
Not a single woman
worth her salt
would take herself off
to sleep in her room
the night you were waked.

EILEEN
My friend, my lamb,
pay no heed to her gossip
that would have me resting
while others watched over you.
It was only the children's want
that kept me from you.
They could not sleep
so I lay down between their heads

to drive off the black shadow
from around their bed.

Pay no heed to lies like hers —
rain in a bucket, nothing but noise.
As if any woman who had kissed your thighs
or run her thumb between your ribs,
whose womb was honeyed
three times by your seed,
could hold back on a night like this
with Art O'Leary's body laid out
since early yesterday.

Morris, you treacherous lout,
I hope your body will suffer
a thousand wounds even worse
than your wounding of Art.
I hope your liver shrivels
and your blood congeals,
your eyeballs itch
and your kneecaps split asunder.
You have taken my husband from me
and I see no one in Ireland
with the guts to make you pay.

Rise up, Art,
my own sweet man.
Straddle your mare
and ride down through Macroom
and on into Inchigeela.
One bottle of wine for the journey over,
another for the journey back,

the way it was in your father's day,
and me with my hair tied up in ribbons
that you brought home for me.

I'd give anything
to have been beside you
when they fired the shot.
I could have smothered it
in the folds of my dress
or the folds of my breasts,
what matter, so long
as you kept going,
my fine horseman
of the lissom hands,
over the brow of the hill.

ART'S SISTER
    I'd give anything
    to have been behind you
    when that shot rang out.
    I could have smothered it
    in the folds of my dress
    or my own flesh
    could have taken it.
    You would have gone free then,
    my golden-haired horseman,
    over the brow of the hill.

EILEEN
    My gold coin, my bounty,

that you should come to this.
It's not much of a fairy-tale ending,
the hero in white cap and coffin,
a hero that fished trout from runnels
and still had enough of the man in him
to savour wine in tinkling halls
among white-breasted women.
You were my marvellous distraction.
Now only these words
stir my blood
and keep me company.

I curse you, Morris,
you treacherous lout.
You have left me fatherless children:
two of them alone in the world
and one still kicking inside me
I fear will never breathe his name.

Dear Art,
when you passed through the gate
it didn't take you long
to turn back
to kiss your fine sons
and your airy wife,
to leave these words
on her tongue forever:
'Eileen, look lively,
steady yourself.
I am leaving the house
and I might not be back.'
To my shame, I smirked

at the big talk
that I'd heard from you so often.

Dear Art,
dear silver-hilted soldier,
rise up and throw off that shroud.
Put on instead your slim-waisted suit,
the gloves that were cut
from the skin of a calf
and your hat of beaver fur.
Here is your whip
and your mare prepared
for the long trek east
on narrow roads
where every tree
will rustle to cool you
and every river
will suck itself in
when you are set to cross.
Men and women will bow
like reeds before you
if they haven't forgotten how.

Husband,
it isn't the dead
of my own family,
my three unravelled babies
or Donal O'Connell
or Conall that drowned
or my sister,
who at little more than twenty
took herself off

across foreign water
to bide time with a queen.
It's none of them
I'm thinking of
and it isn't on them
I am calling,
but on my own Art,
murdered by treacherous hands:
Art of the sun,
like a mantle around him,
Art of the shapely words,
Art of the majestic mare,
cut down like some
bothersome thistle
on the verge at Carriginima.
I curse that place:
until they saw me
crazed with grief,
its thin-lipped,
mill-black women
didn't shed a single tear.

My calf,
my Art O'Leary,
son of Conor, son of Céadach,
son of Laoiseach O'Leary:
from as far west as the Geeragh
and east, up to the hills
where wild berries speckle,
nuts bead the branches
and apples spill
like ripe sunlight

all over our young day —
it wouldn't take me by surprise
if bonfires were lit on O'Leary turf
and in Ballingeary
and Gougane Barra
for the streaming horseman
who exhausted the hunt
flagging after him from Grenagh,
the hounds still limping back.

My sloe-eyed lover,
what went wrong yesterday?
I thought, when I bought
that suit for you, it would slip
between you and all harm,
so your skin and bones inside it
would home to lie with mine.

ART'S SISTER
My dear,
the pet of our whole family.
Eighteen new mothers
were paid to nurse you,
paid in cows and mares and sows,
in land and coins and satin bows,
all for suckling from their breasts
your own plump, well-kissed lips.

Brother, my brother,
though I wasn't with you
and I didn't lead a horde

to honour you,
don't think less of me:
it was only because
I'm unable to stir them
from rooms without windows
and graves without doors.

If it wasn't for the smallpox,
spotted fever and plague
that have the country addled,
a clamour of horsemen
would set the roads ringing
to get to your funeral,
my white-handed Art.

Dear brother,
friend to wild horsemen
who'd course through the valley
until you'd lead them back
to your high-windowed hall
where knives were whetted
and tables spread
with pork from pigs
that had never been bested,
and ribs from only
the sweet-tempered lambs,
with oats by the bushel
that would make a nag giddy,
never mind the sleek stallions
of your wild horse-boys
who could eat all around them
and stay for a week,

who could stable their horses
and never be asked
to offer so much as a shilling
to put towards their keep.

My pet, my little goose,
last night as I lay in bed in Cork
I dreamt that the moon-white walls of home
were withering around us,
that our childhood had dried up
and left us bewildered,
that the birds were not singing,
and even your little whelp
had stopped his fretting in the yard.
I was alone. You'd gone on.
Then they found you
at the single furze
with no priest beside you,
but an old woman over you
with a filthy, ragged coat.
Art, my pet, my darling lad,
death had already
soaked clean through
the white shirt you were wearing.

My golden lad,
you were gorgeous always
in your hand-woven stockings
and knee-high boots,
your Carolina hat,
a whip in your hand
to put manners on a gelding.

I often saw girls from good families
twitch at the tether when you'd pass.

EILEEN
   Husband,
   when you rode your gallantry
   into a fortress town
   the shopkeepers' wives
   in their frippery
   would practically fall over.
   They could see as well as I
   what their husbands could never,
   that you'd be a masterful lover
   with the reins in your hands,
   leading them on through secret thickets
   into the wild country.

   And that you'd be a vigorous father
   unless something angered you,
   but that would be rare and, anyway,
   a man with so much fire in him
   would have to flame up now and then.
   Not that it matters anyway,
   now the blaze of your life has been doused.

   God knows, the very cap on my head,
   the silk on my thigh,
   the buckle on my shoe,
   the sheets on my bed
   and the brown mare's bridle —
   I will spend the lot,

if I have to, at law,
and I will sail across the sea
to make my case to the King.
If he will not listen
I'll come back here alone
to the door of the black-blooded villain
who had my husband murdered.

If my own family could hear me
back in Derrynane
the men would set out on their horses
and the women would come
in their mourning gowns
to stand with me
over your stretched body,
to wet your cheeks
with tears.

My heart goes out instead
to those fair mill women
who, I have to say now,
rhymed elegantly
over my horseman
of the brown mare
as he lay on the verge
of Carriginima.
Not that it matters anyway,
my own words didn't rouse him.

The curse of my heart goes out to you,
outlaw, Seán Cooney,
who took a pittance to inform on Art.

If it was only money you wanted
you could have come to me.
I'd have given whatever you needed —
even a sturdy horse to bear you through
Art's funeral
when you had to escape.
Or a herd of cows
or ewes in lamb
or a secret for bleaching linen;
even a suit of my own Art's
though it would have been too big, I see,
for your puny, knock-kneed body.

My white-gloved horseman,
now your hand has been stayed,
may it act slyly against Baldwin,
that miserable, grasping, mean-spirited dolt.
For handing over your treasured brown mare
and for going against me
may he rot in hell
and his six children too,
though maybe not Máire,
since we are blood.

Máire, dear sister,
I'd stand up for you
and I'll love you tomorrow,
and again the day after.
Not that it matters anyway.
Your husband did me a great wrong.
Take away now out of here
him and his retinue.

Dear Mother,
you have kept your house wisely
and husbanded well.
If it has been a good twelve years
since I stood on the other side of your door
it isn't down to any squabble or feud;
it's only that I had a busy house
of my own to manage
and all its goings on to tend to:
honey to filter,
milk to skim,
hams that had to be cured.
But I'll visit you soon
if you'll send word
of a welcome back
for Art's ruined wife
and Art's two ruined sons.

And one of those sons
I will send abroad
to try his hand at Latin
though we'd planned a different story
that would have had him
lord over towns
where the English
would have looked up to him,
being his father's son.

Dear friends
of the famed O'Leary clan,
of Art from Gougane Barra,
of Tadhg of the odd breastplates,

and of the headstrong, peerless Art
who was my loved and doting husband
until the verge of the road
and his enemies undid him,
neither of which
cared so much as a whit
for all that he was
generous and handsome
and so brave.

But to all of you weeping
I say, 'Wait and see:
Art O'Leary will be along any minute.
He'll call for a drink
to drown thirst and sorrow,
pay for it with his own money,
and then take himself off
to the shadow school —
not to be learning
or trying new tunes —
but to lie down with clay
and stones and bones
in an overcome abbey.'

My love, my husband,
your corn may thrive
but your cows still need milking
and your children are calling for you.
Rise up now and come with me
to our white house
with its kitchens of plenty
and brightly-voiced halls,

to where trees will bear us ruby apples
and wild strawberries
will crimson our tongues,
to where bees will hum like hooded monks
when you bid them take a turn around
the thriving, glossy holly tree
you planted when little Conor was born
and another then for Fiach.

Rise up now and come with me,
for the weight of sorrow
across my heart
will not lift
unless you pitch it off.
It is like a chest
with stones in it
and I am very much afraid
that its rusted lock
and fastened latch
will never know a key.